3rd Grade Cursive Handwriting Workbook 3rd

Practice Level One
Letters & Words
Age 8+

R
r
Rex
rare
raccoon
raspberry

Tips for Teaching Handwriting

~~**Short and sweet.** Plan for a 10-15 minute teaching session each day with your child. This includes the time for supervised practice with you. Keep sessions short and focused on the correct formation of each letter with the proper pencil grip. Learn one letter a day at first. This helps them learn how to make it correctly. if your child is doing well you may be able to do more than one page or letter as you keep going.

~~**Measured and Monitored.** During handwriting time with your child, watch them work. Remind them of the steps for making the letter if you see them writing in the wrong direction. Show them how to make the letter on your own piece of paper or by writing in the air. Then ask them to think about the steps and try again. Avoid erasing. Just have them move over and make a new letter.

~~**Letters Make Words, Words Make Sentences,** Sentences Make Paragraphs, and Copywork Makes Good Handwriting. Once your child can make the letters, the next step is to copy words and sentences. Next they will copy paragraphs. Continued daily practice will keep developing more complex handwriting skills and brain processes.

~~**Practice makes perfect. Perfect sense, that is.** Practice handwriting everyday, even after your child has learned all the letters. Just like riding a bike or playing the piano, the more you practice, the better your will be at it. Regular handwriting practice makes handwriting automatic. Research shows that if handwriting is automatic, the child can focus on WHAT they are writing about instead of HOW to write the letters in the answers. This helps your child learn at a higher level, especially when they learn cursive.

~~**Small Time Investment with Big Return.** Put in the 10-15 minutes daily now to teach your child how to write correctly and neatly. Then follow up with daily practice year round so handwriting will become automatic for your child and they can do copywork independently. When your child practices handwriting, those brain benefits spread to learning other subjects. Daily handwriting practice is the gift that keeps on giving to your child's learning in all subjects.

FAQs
Frequently Asked Questions

1. Do we really need to practice handwriting everyday?

Yes! If you want your child to have greater success in school and reap the brain benefits of handwriting which affects all subjects, you need to practice daily. The good news is that it's not as hard as you think. Focus on handwriting practice everyday for just a short time as a separate subject for about 10-15 minutes. It is not the amount of practice that makes good handwriting. It is the amount of CORRECT practice that counts. These concentrated handwriting sessions can make great progress if you do them everyday. Handwriting practice also helps your child to read and learn all subjects easier so it's a Win-Win.

2. What else can I do?

At Peachy Keen Products we teach the old fashioned way they learn it! We believe in the tried and true traditional techniques for learning. We know that kids need more practice than just a single workbook page for handwriting. Use our matching blank paper workbook for the same grade. If your child is having trouble with a letter, do some extra practice on the blank pages but still keep your daily handwriting sessions short and focused. It's okay if some letters take more time to master. One time through this workbook is not enough to learn all the letters well.

Practice makes progress. All kids need lots of practice. Don't stop handwriting practice once your child knows how to make all the letters. Once they know the letters, then they copy words, then sentences and then short paragraphs. Keep moving up. You should see their handwriting improve for all subjects if you keep doing a daily short handwriting practice.

Check out our other workbooks and virtual home school planners by searching for Peachy Keen Products on Amazon. Please feel free to email us anytime at info@peachykeenproducts.com with any questions Follow Peachy Keen Products on Pinterest for teaching ideas and freebies for lots of different subjects and ages.

**~Experience Low Stress-Teaching Success
with Peachy Keen Products!~**

Hey! Why is the inside of this book turned sideways!?

~Little hands need bigger spaces for better practice.~

That's why Peachy Keen Workbooks use age-appropriate line spacing and horizontal orientation.

Traditionally all handwriting papers were horizontal through the 3rd grade including beginning cursive. Vertical paper was started in 4th grade with wide ruled notebook paper after the child had learned how to write correctly and was then able to write smaller. Many of the current handwriting papers and books are vertical and sized too small, too soon. Having to use smaller lined paper before a child has practiced sufficiently on bigger paper is frustrating and often results in an illegible paper or an unsuccessful experience.

PEACHY KEEN
PRODUCTS

**~Experience Low Stress–Teaching Success
with Peachy Keen Products!~**

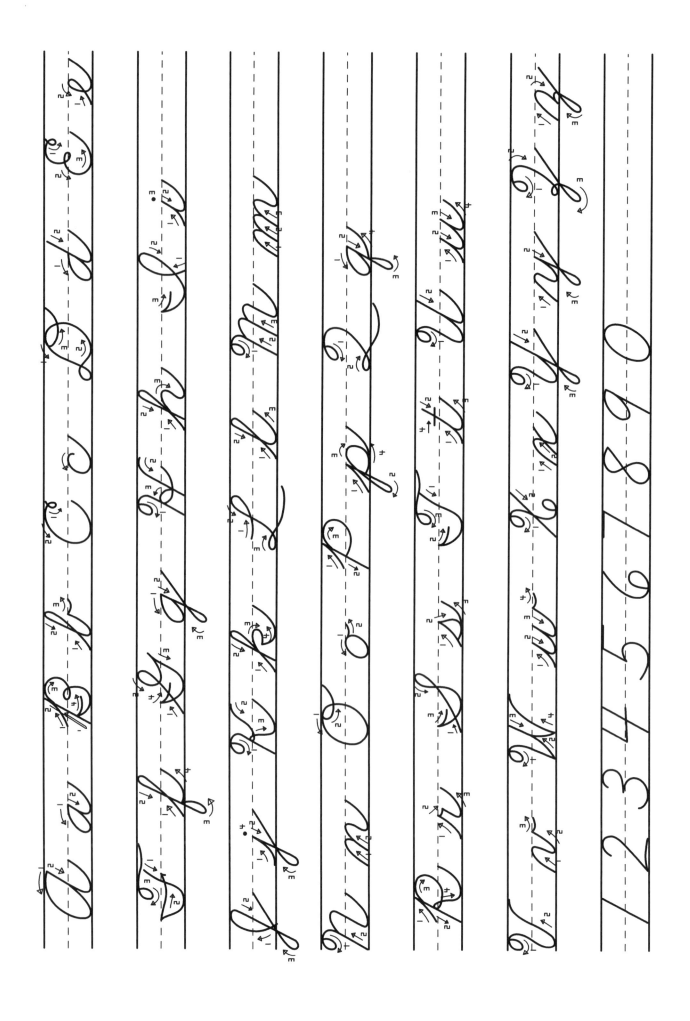

Third Grade
Cursive Practice
Lowercase A-Z

Directions for Letter Practice Pages

1. Take your time. Think about the steps for each letter.
2. Trace the arrow letters with your finger.
3. Trace the first row of dotted letters with your pencil.
4. For the next 2 rows, write the letter in between the printed letters.
5. For the last 2 rows, write the letter on the row at least 4 times or more.
6. Find your best work on the page and put a star or happy face by it.
7. Don't forget to color the pictures. You can do them first or last.
8. Do your best. :o)

~Experience Low Stress-Teaching Success with Peachy Keen Products!~

~We Teach Kids the Old-Fashioned Way... They LEARN IT!~

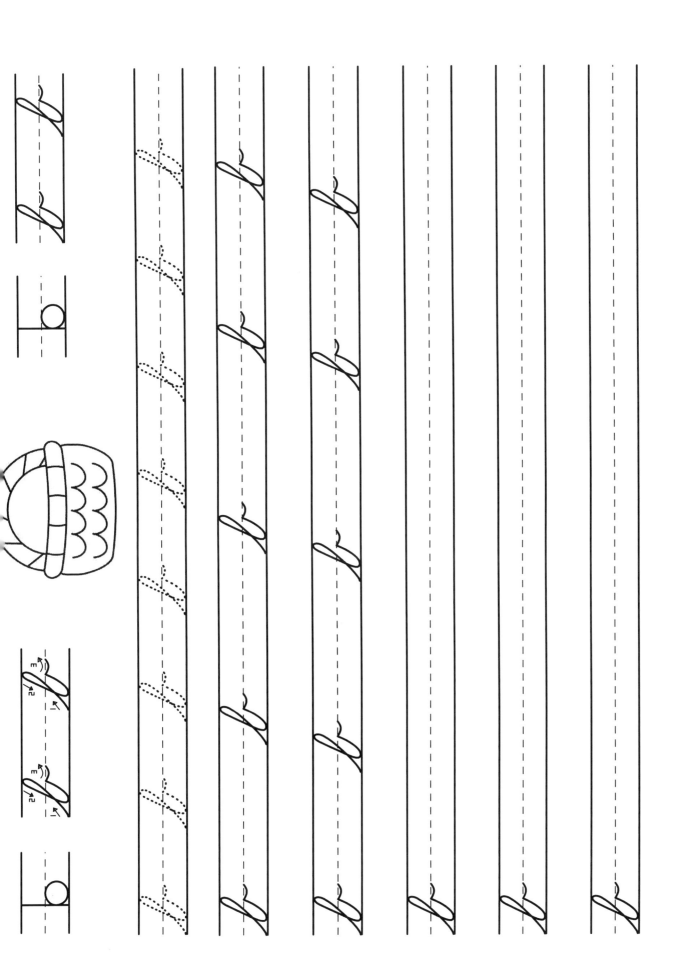

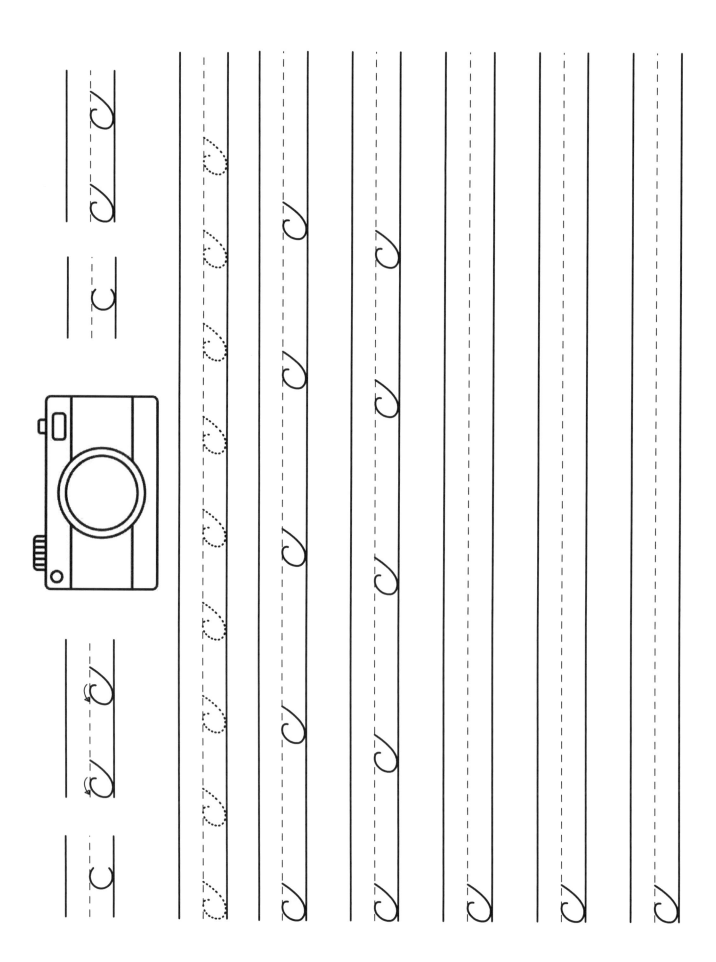

d d

d

d d

d d

d d

d d

d d

d

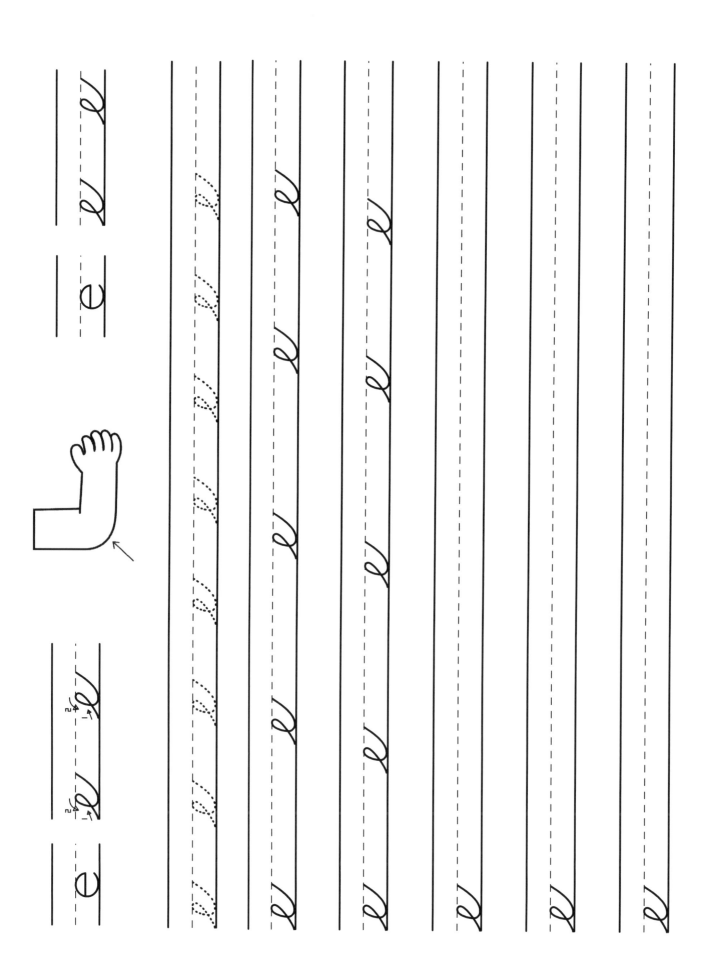

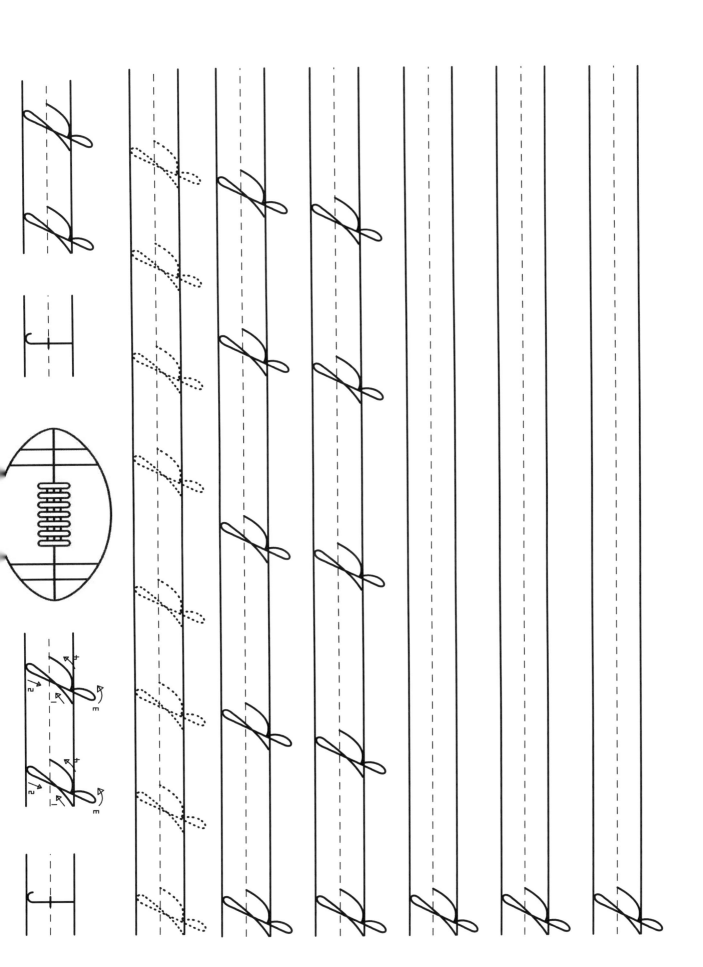

g g g 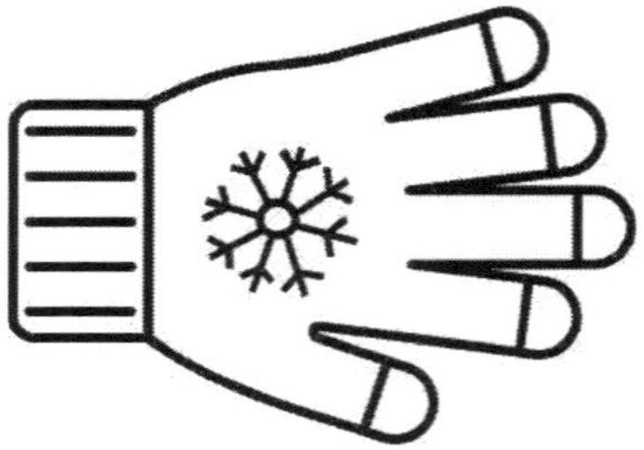 g g g

g g g g g g g g

g g g g g

g g g g g

g

g

g

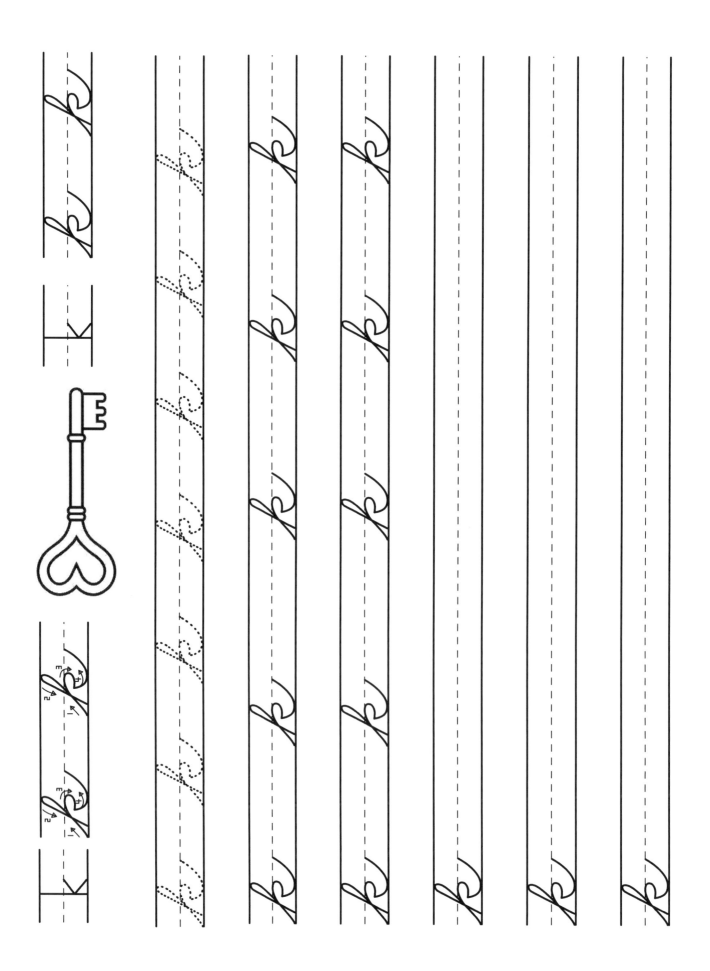

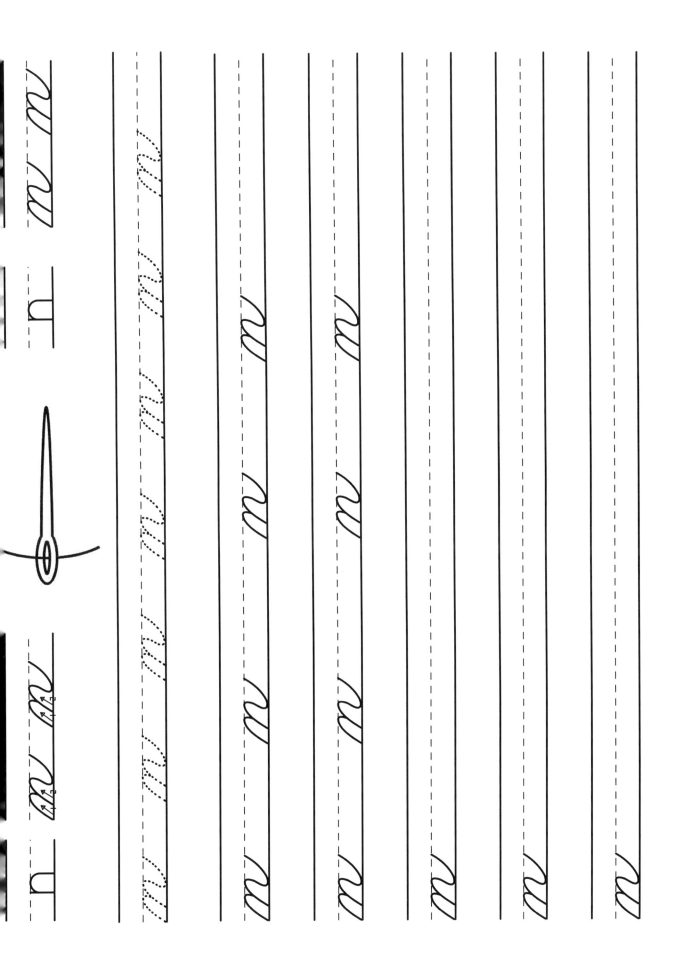

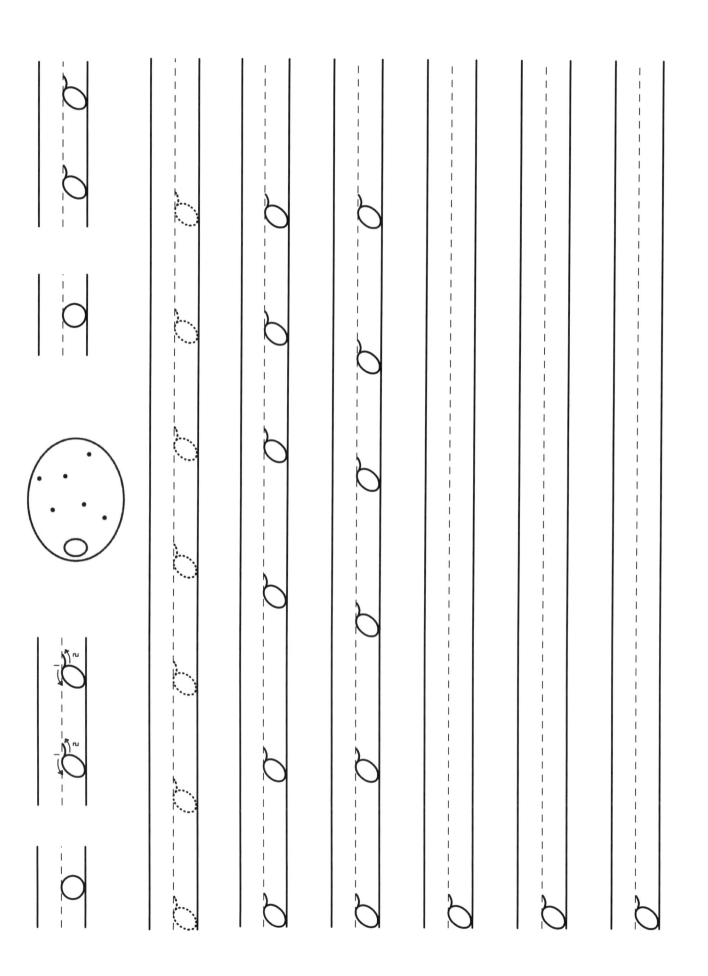

p *p* *p* 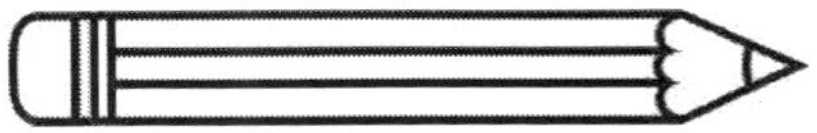 p *p* *p*

p *p* *p* *p* *p* *p*

p *p* *p* *p* *p*

p *p* *p* *p* *p*

p

p

p

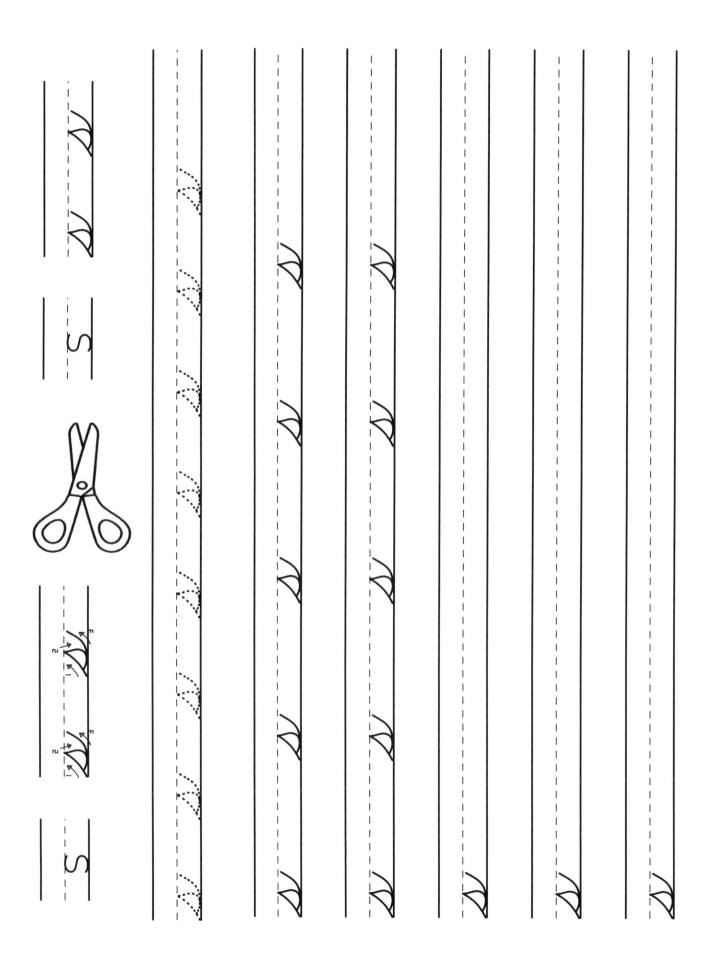

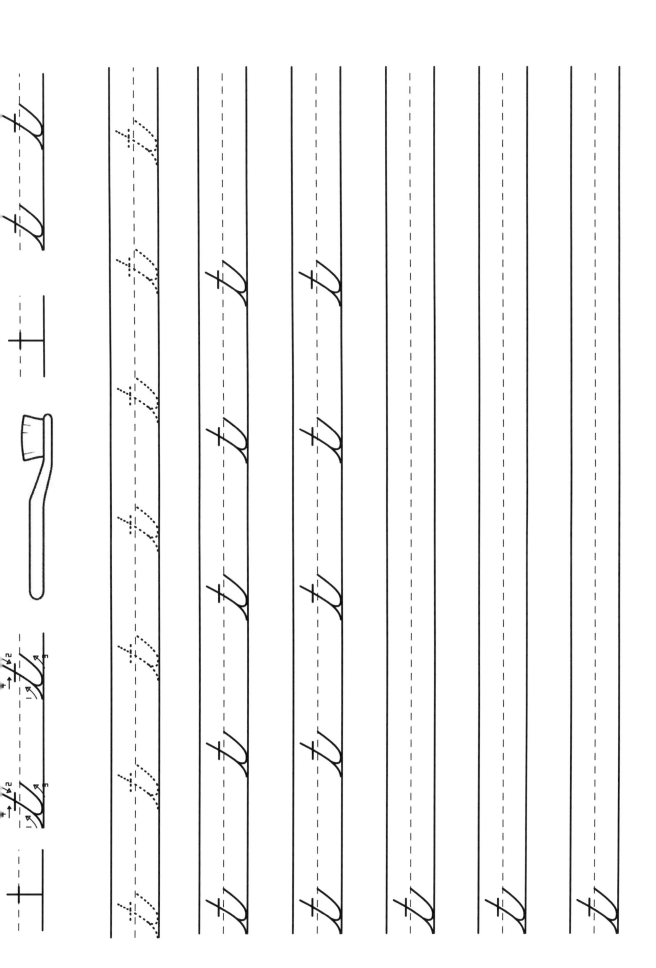

У у у 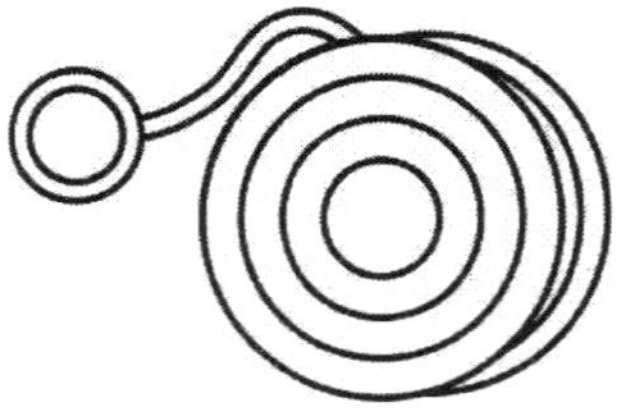 У у у

у у у у у у

у у у у у

у у у у у

у

у

у

Z z z

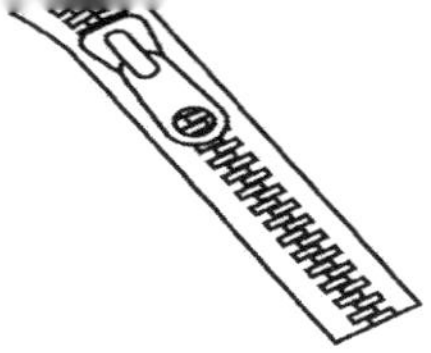

Z z z

z z z z z z z z z z

z z z z z

z z z z z

z

z

z

Third Grade
Cursive Practice
Capitals A-Z

Directions for Letter Practice Pages

1. Take your time. Think about the steps for each letter.
2. Trace the arrow letters with your finger.
3. Trace the first row of dotted letters with your pencil.
4. For the next 2 rows, write the letter in between the printed letters.
5. For the last 2 rows, write the letter on the row at least 4 times or more.
6. Find your best work on the page and put a star or happy face by it.
7. Don't forget to color the pictures. You can do them first or last.
8. Do your best. :o)

~Experience Low Stress-Teaching Success with Peachy Keen Products!~

~We Teach Kids the Old-Fashioned Way... They LEARN IT!~

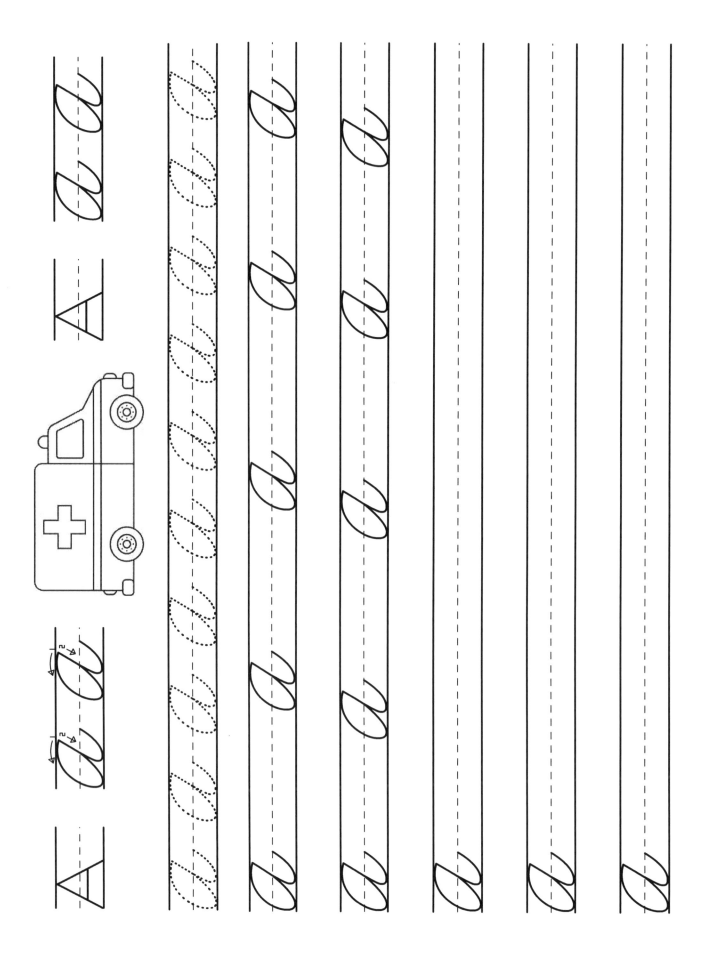

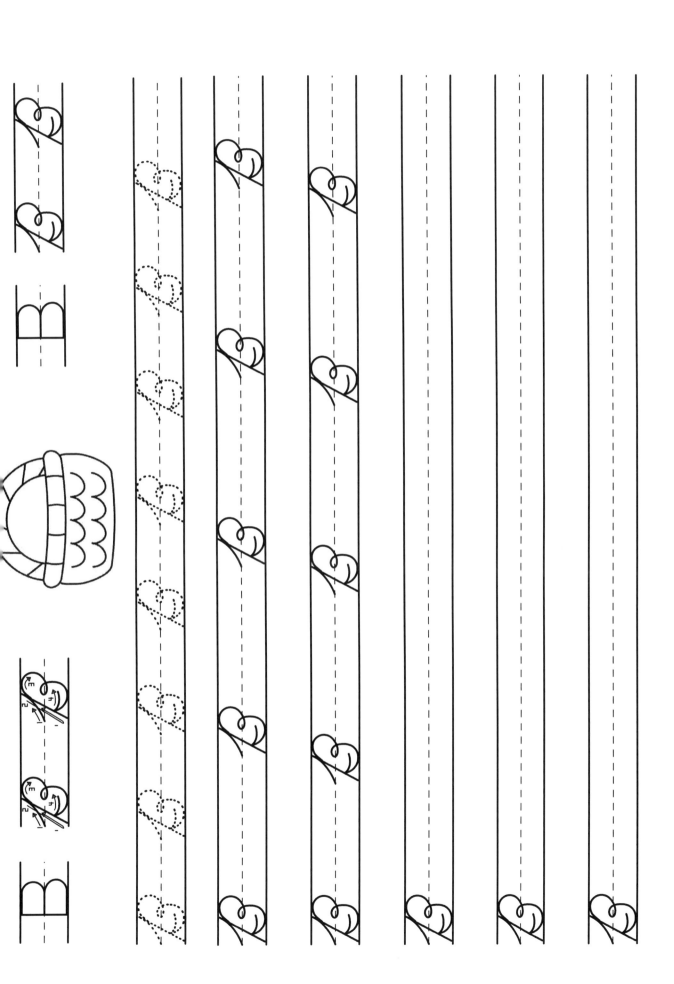

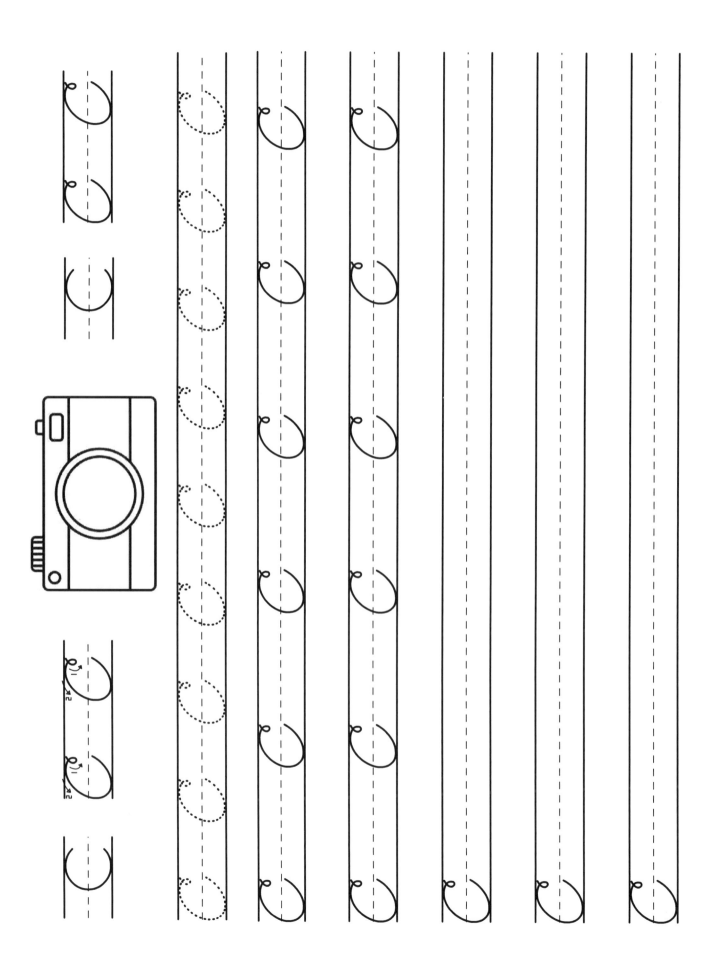

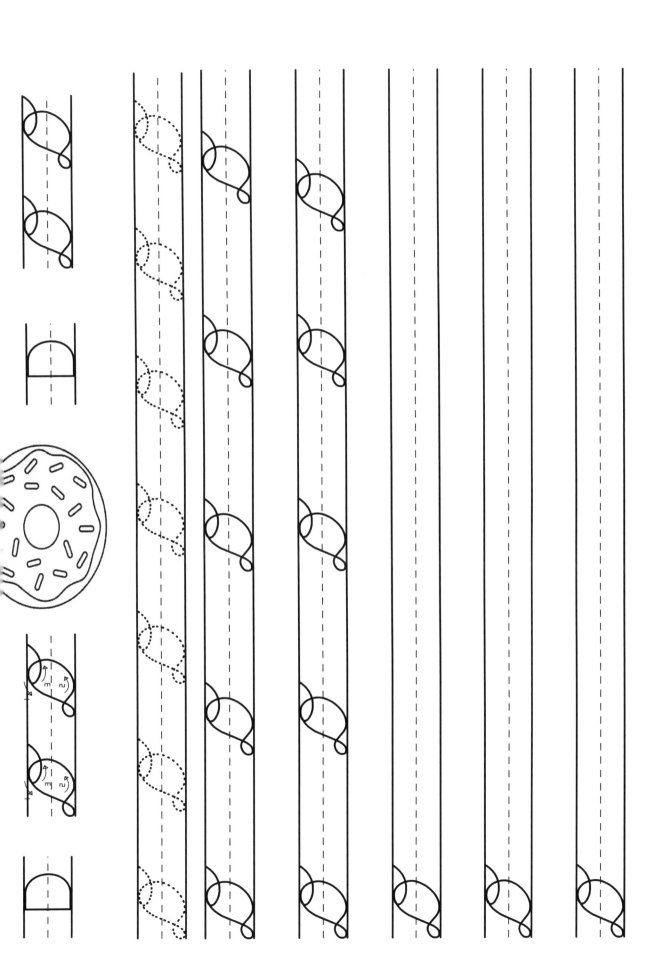

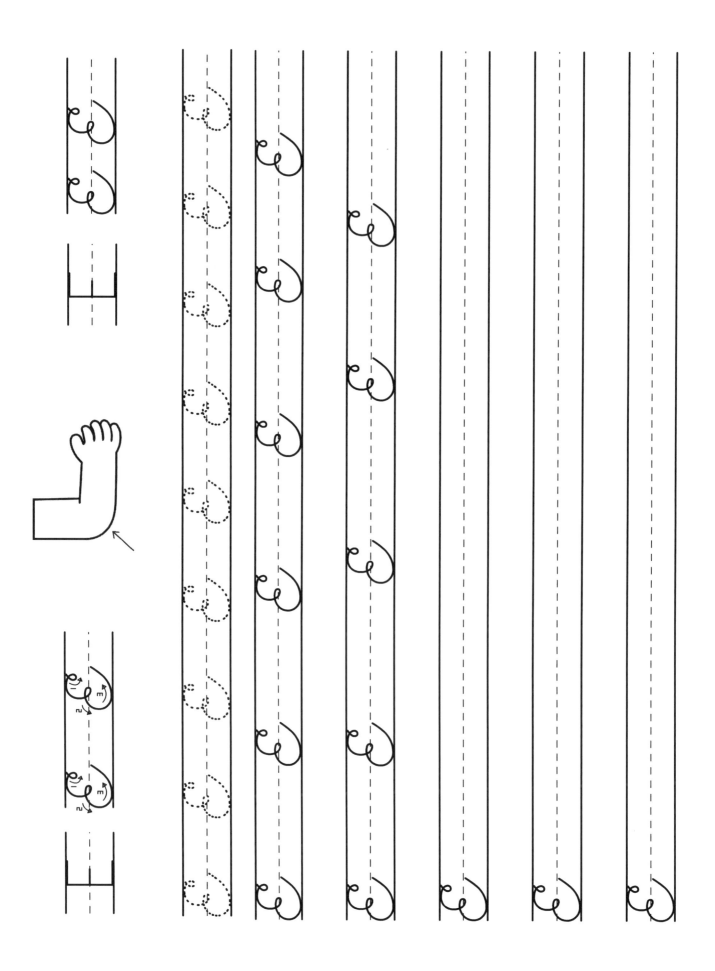

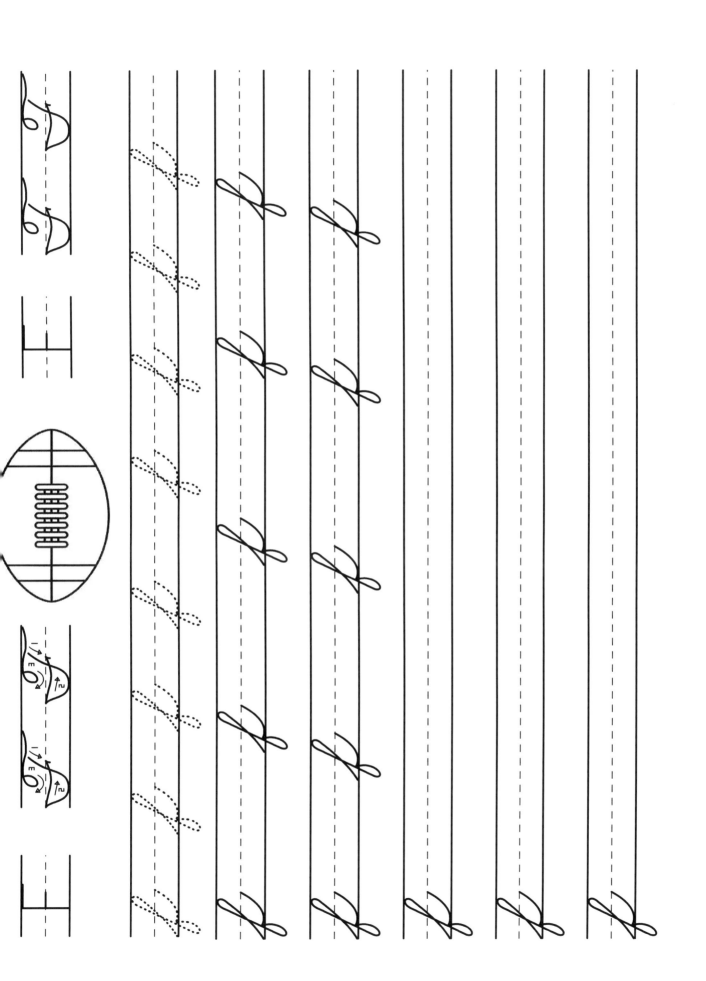

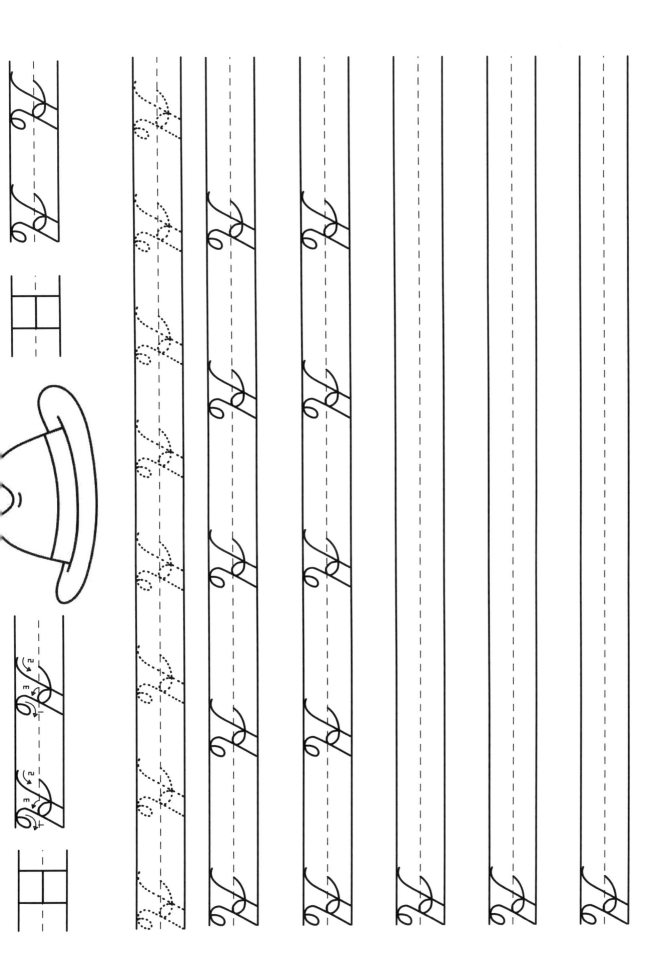

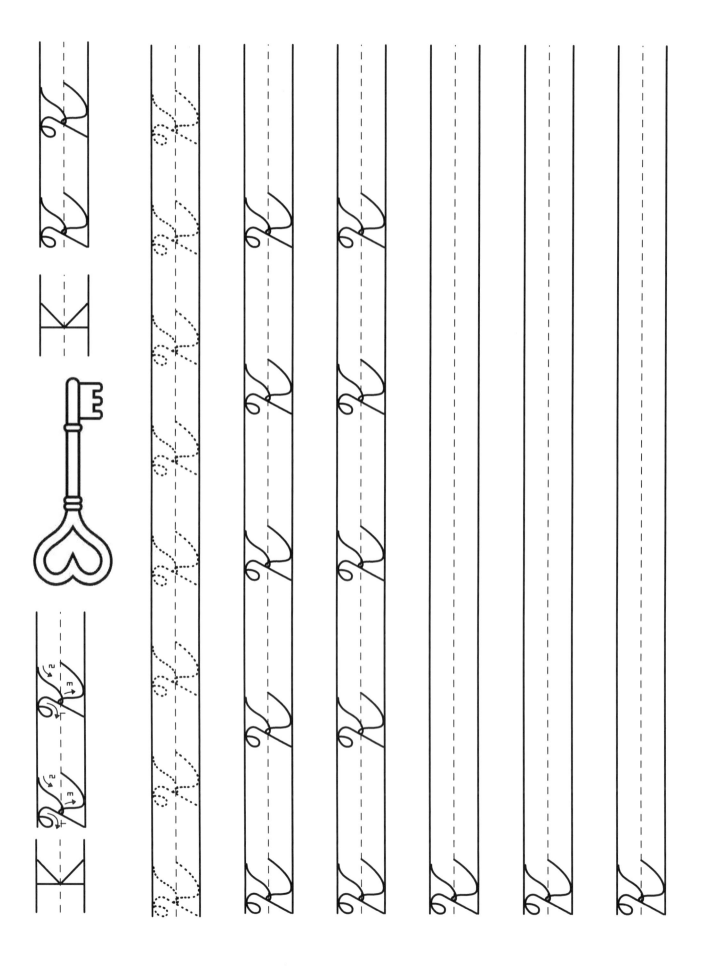

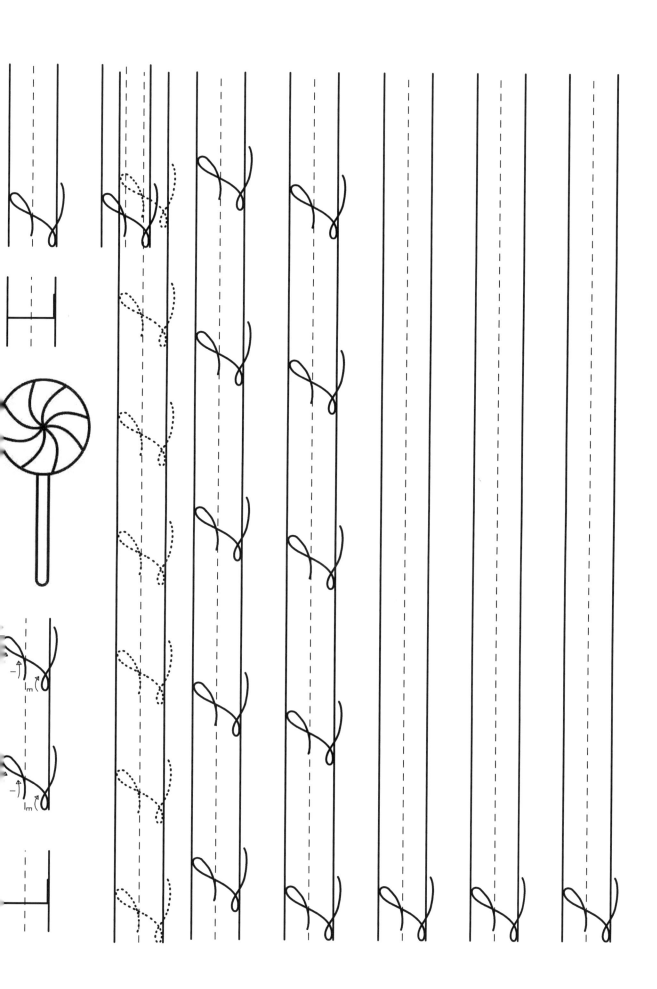

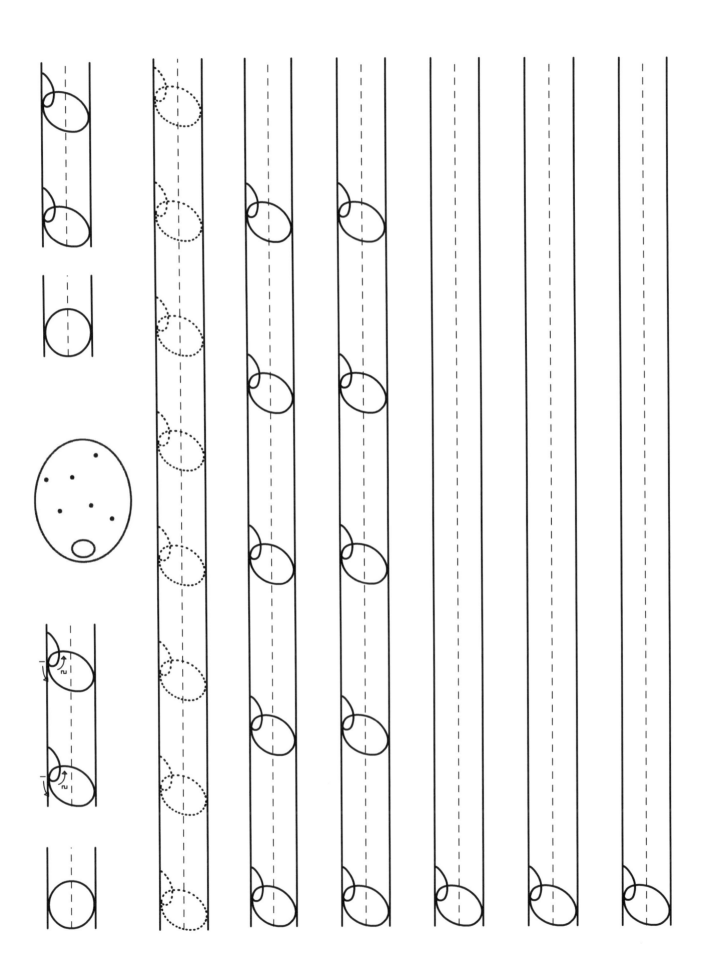

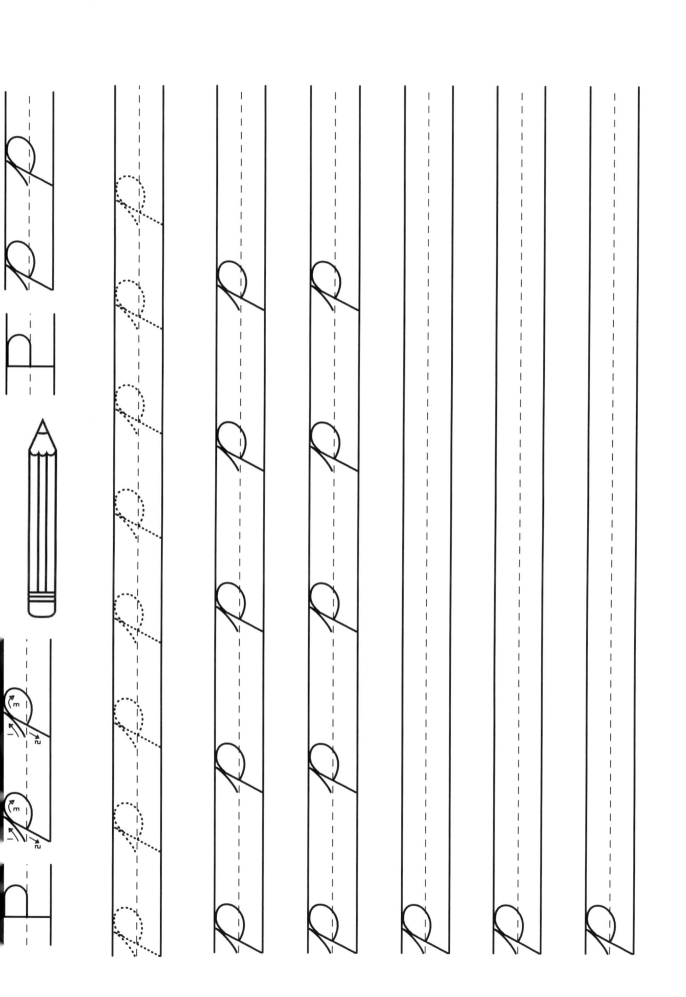

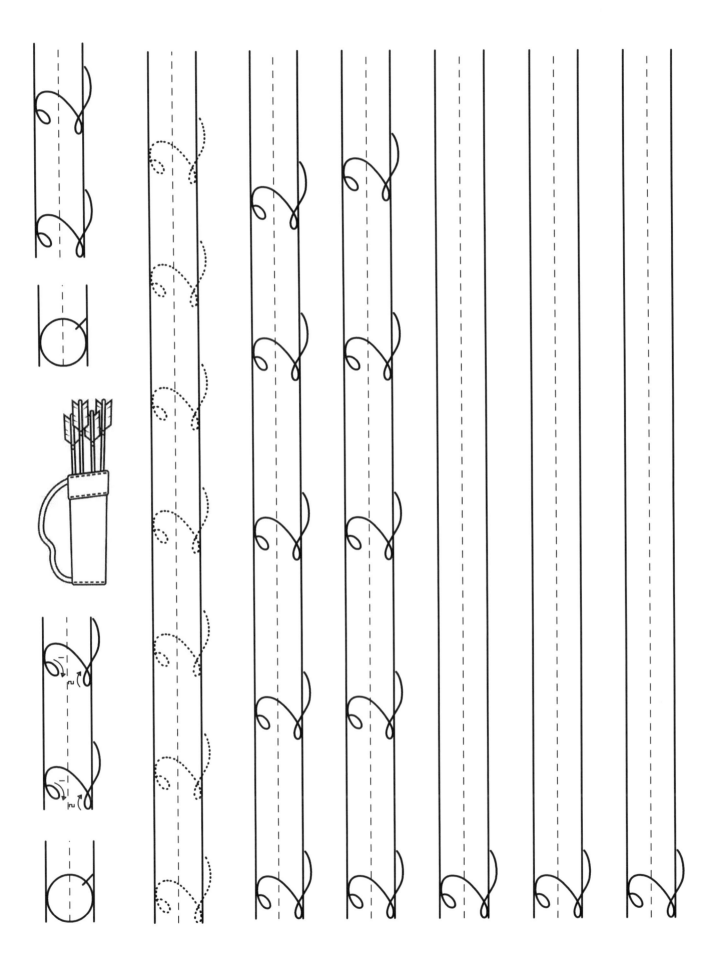

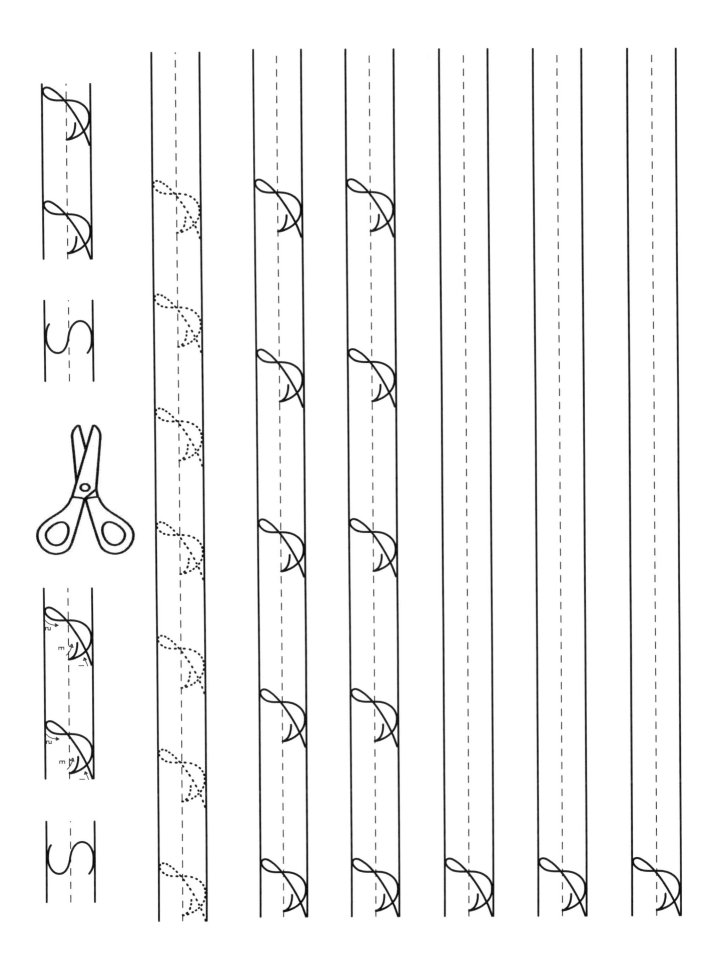

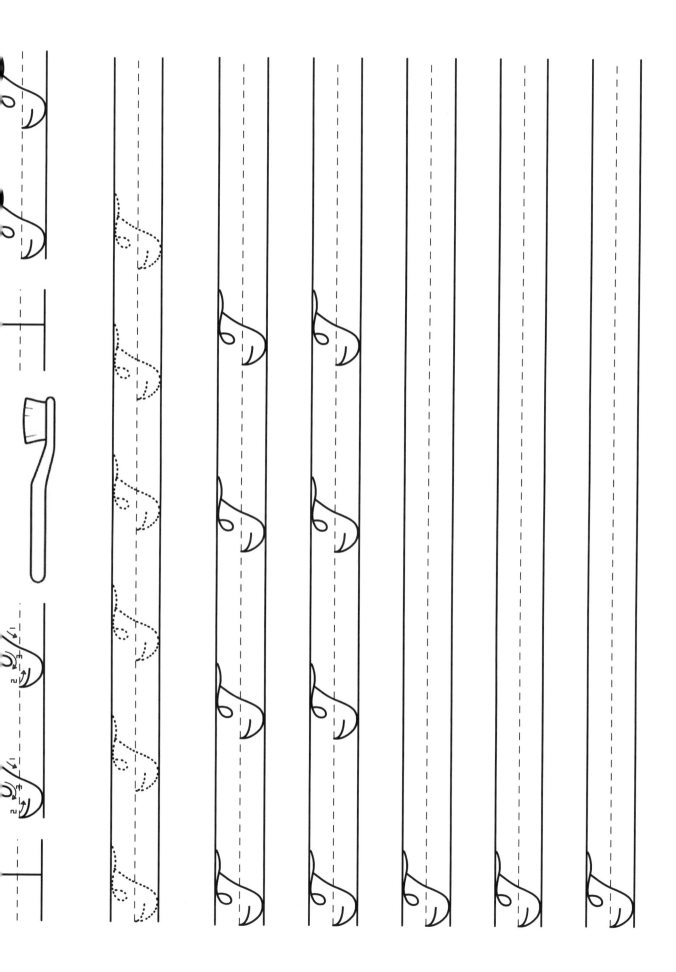

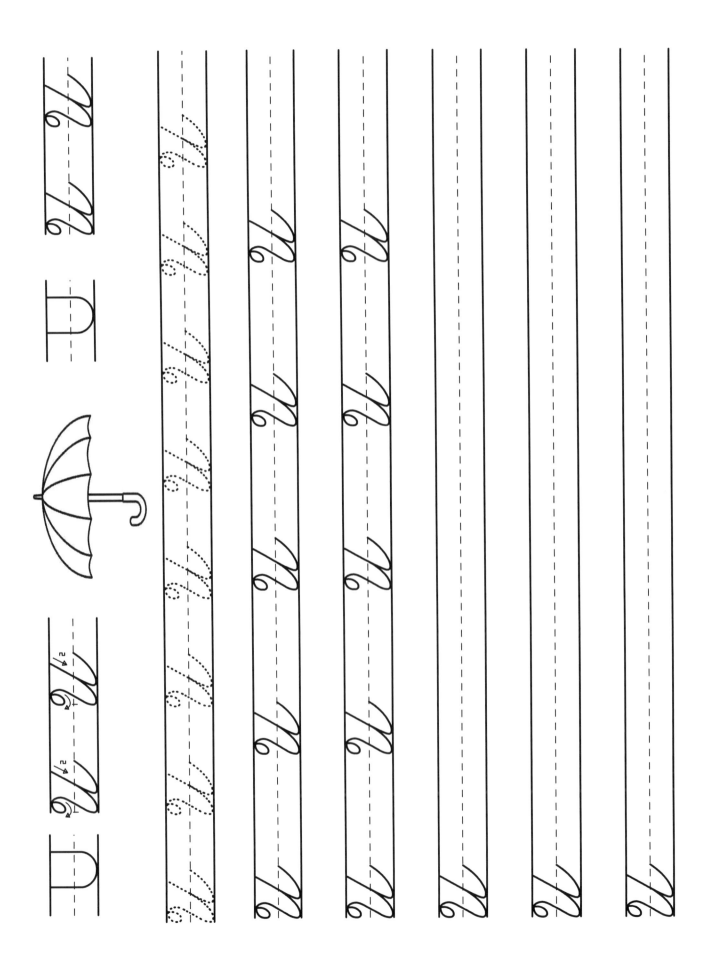

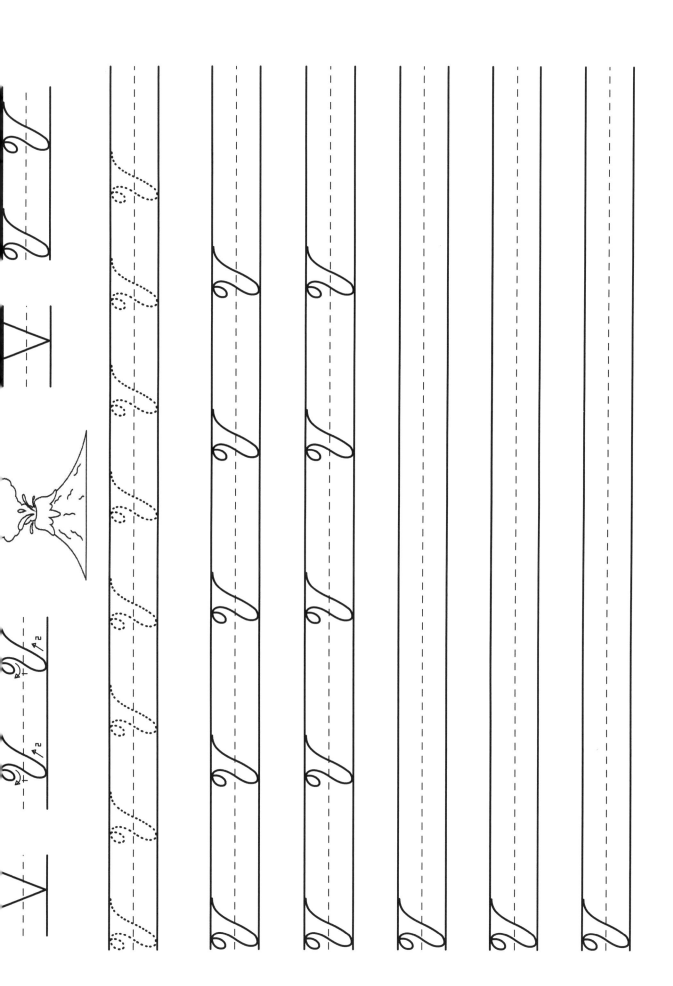

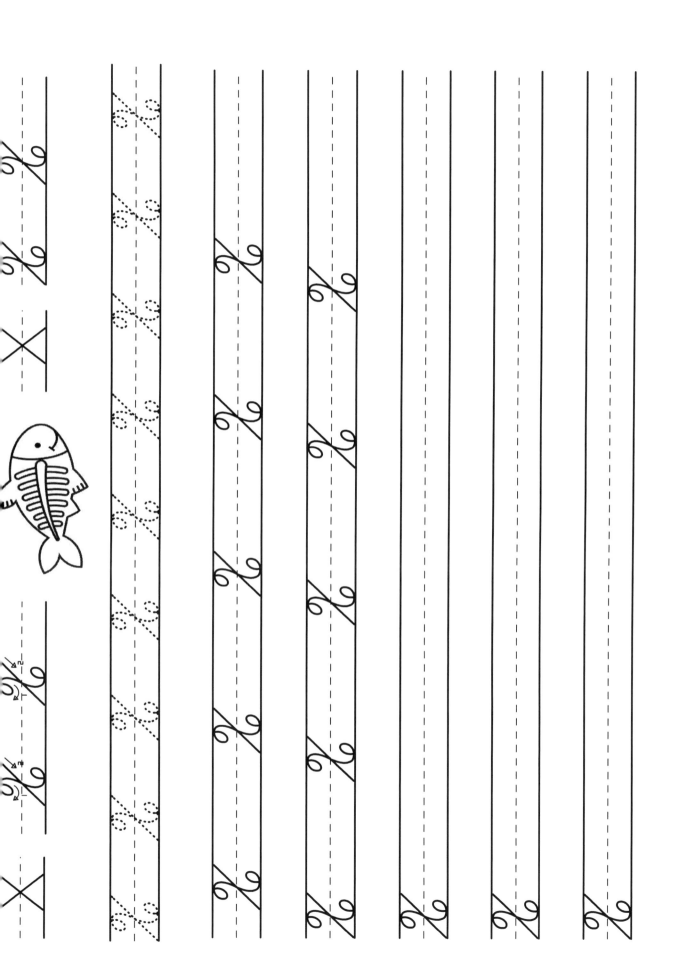

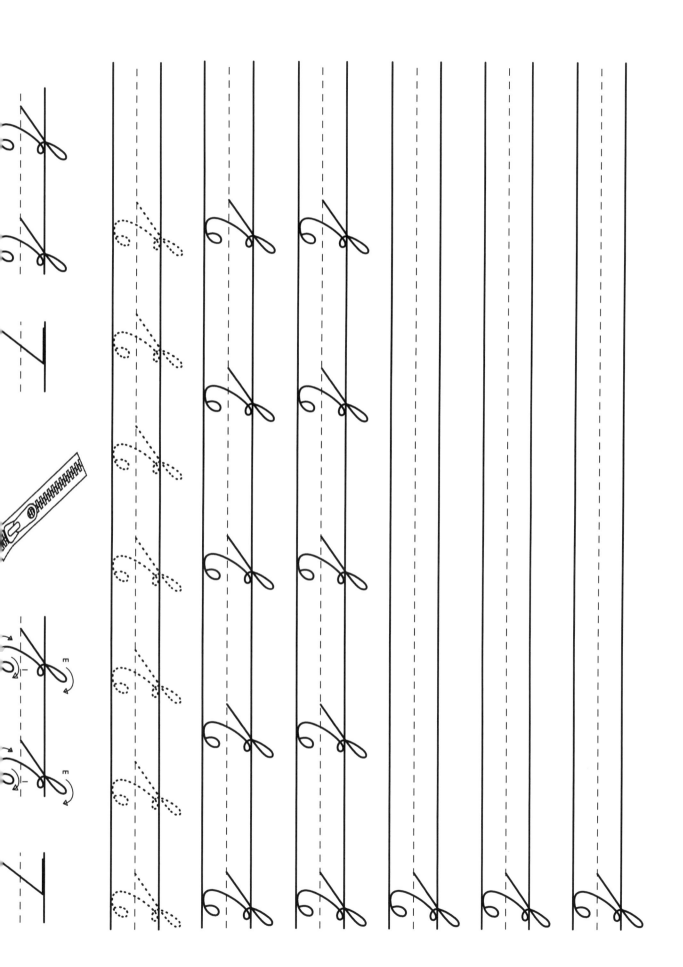

Third Grade Cursive Word Practice A-Z

Directions for Letter Practice Pages

1. Take your time. Think about the steps for each letter before you start.
2. Write the capital letter on the row at least 4 times or more.
3. Write the lowercase letter on the row at least 4 times or more.
4. Look at the word and think about how to write the letters in the word.
5. Copy the word on each row at least 2 times or more.
6. Find your best work on the page and put a star or happy face by it.
7. Don't forget to color the pictures. You can do them first or last.
8. Do your best. :o)

~Experience Low Stress-Teaching Success with Peachy Keen Products!~

~We Teach Kids the Old-Fashioned Way... They LEARN IT!~

l

a

Andy

always

anchor

airplane

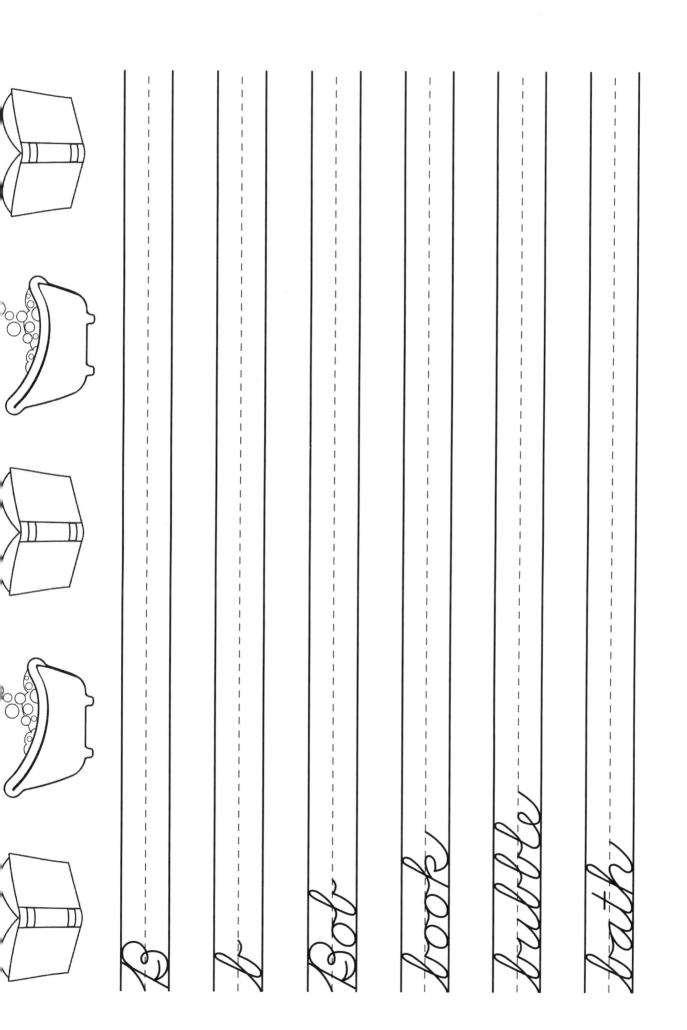

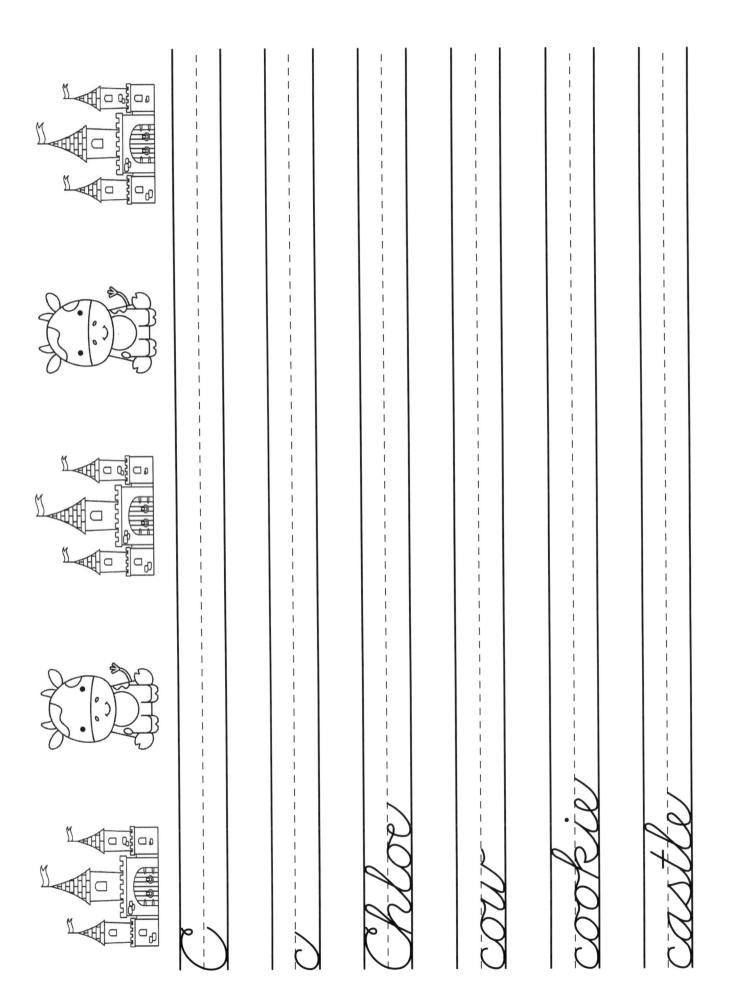

C

c

Chloe

cow

cookie

castle

D

d

Dave

didn't

doors

dolphin

e

l

ed

every

eagle

eggplant

F f Frank frog fluffy flamingo

G

g

Grace

good

goat

grass

H

h

Hannah

high

hobby

hippo

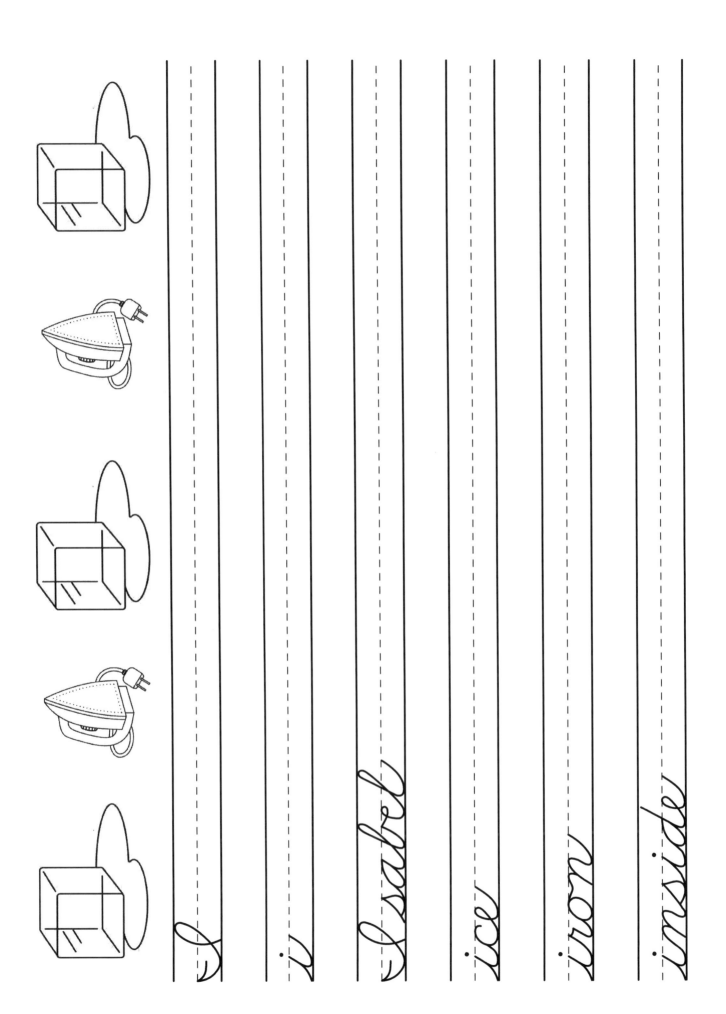

I i

Isabel

ice

iron

inside

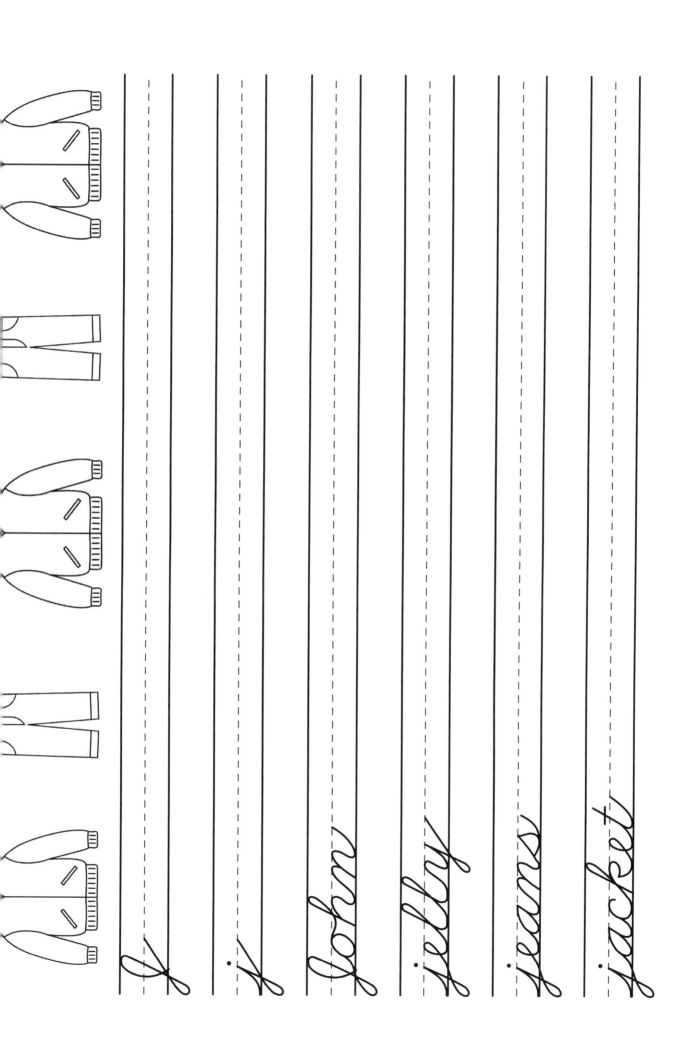

J

j

John

jelly

jeans

jacket

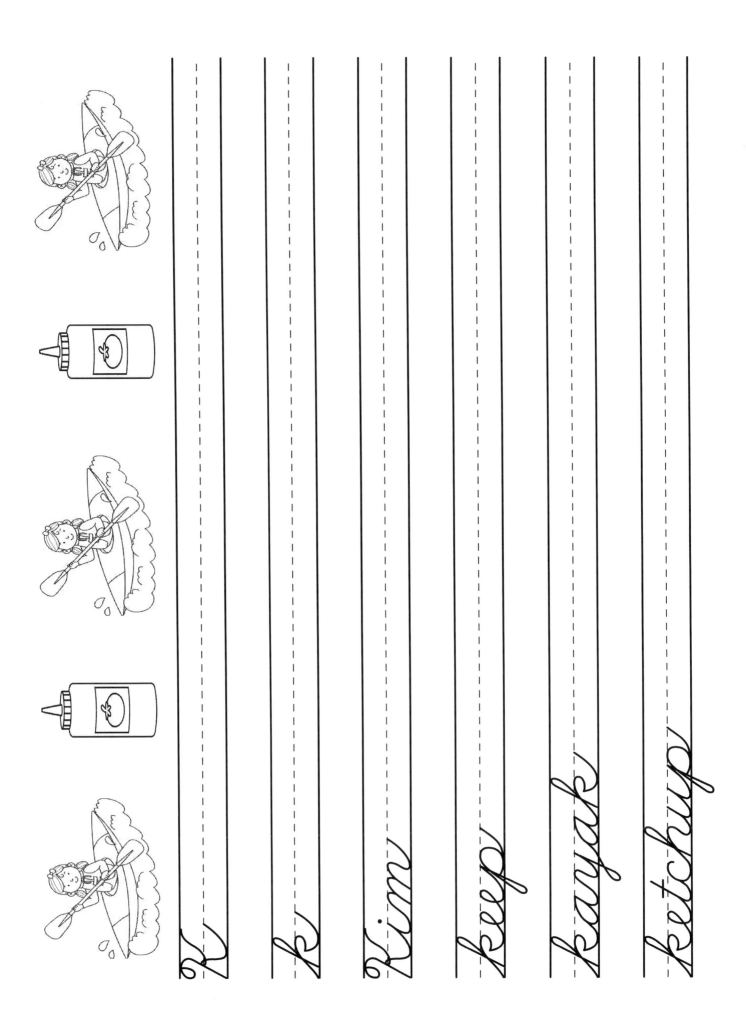

𝒦

𝓀

Kim

keep

kayak

ketchup

$\mathcal{L}$ l $\mathcal{L}eo$ $little$ $leaf$ $lizard$

m

m

matt

map

mermaid

mumble

N

n

nancy

net

narwhal

noodles

O

o

Olaf

out

onion

octopus

P

p

Pete

puppy

penguin

pineapple

2

9

Quentin

quiz

quarter

question

R r Ren rare raccoon raspberry

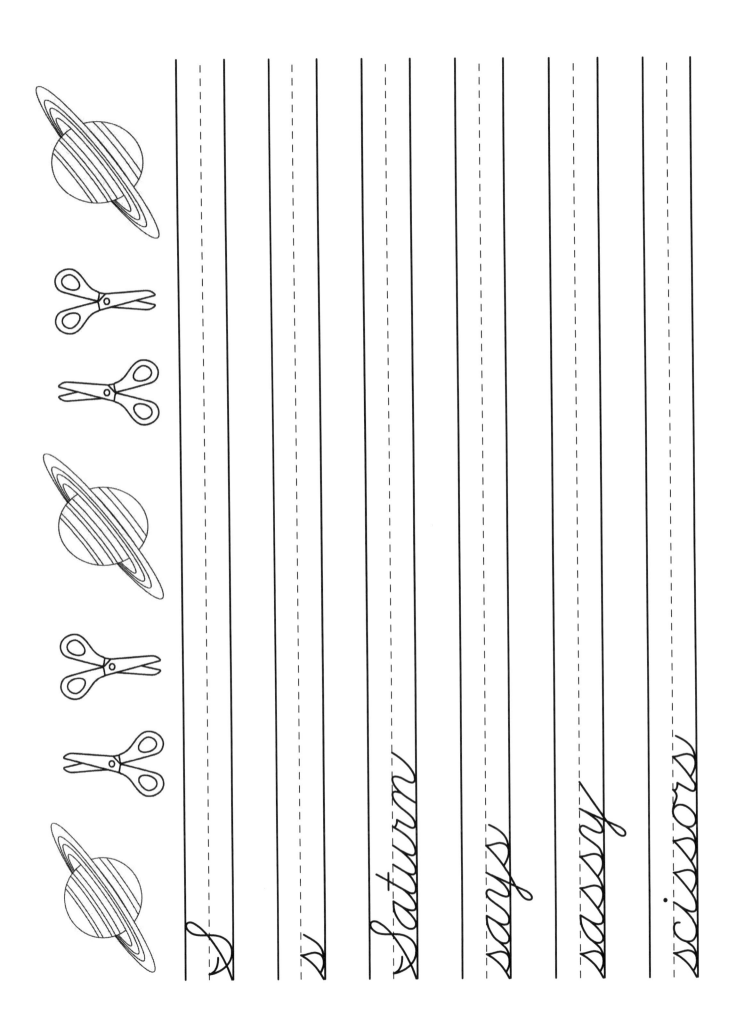

Saturn

says

sassy

scissors

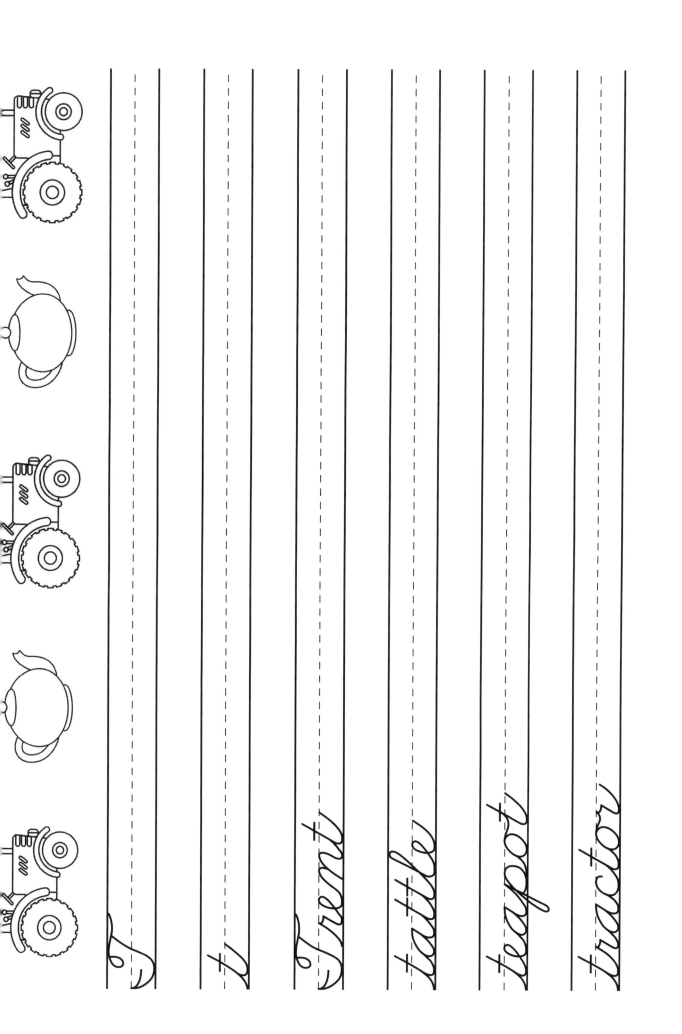

T t

Trent

tattle

teapot

tractor

$\mathcal{U}$

u

Utah

ugly

upset

underground

$\mathcal{V}$

$\mathcal{v}$

$\mathcal{Vivian}$

$\mathcal{very}$

$\mathcal{vest}$

$\mathcal{vultures}$

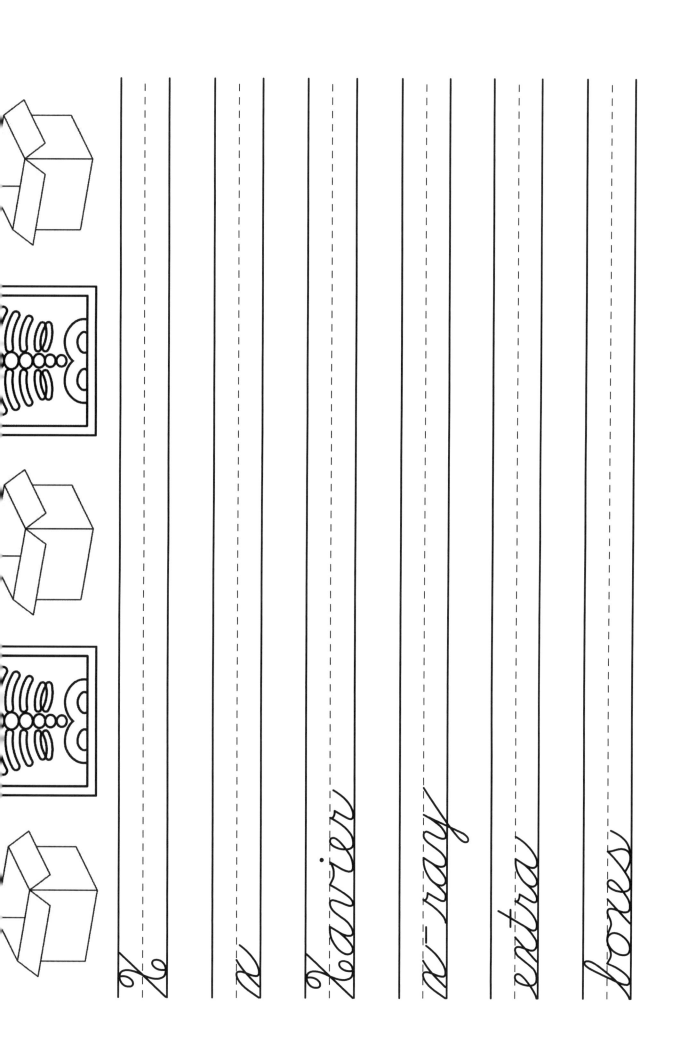

X x

x

Xavier

x-ray

extra

boxes

Y y Yvette yams yellow yarns

Quick Cursive ABC Practice

Write the cursive alphabet by connecting all the letters. Use two lines if needed.

abcdefghijklmnopqrstuvwxyz

abcdefghijklmnopqrstuvwxyz

Name:

1 2 3 4 5 6 7 8 9 0

1 2 3 4 5 6 7 8 9 0

1 2 3 4 5 6 7 8 9 0

1 2 3 4 5 6 7 8 9 0

Made in the USA
Middletown, DE
21 August 2024